GET TO THE
POINT

ULTIMATE GUIDE TO REACHING
YOUR DIVINE POTENTIAL

Gregory Ford

Pastor Dan & Darlene Betzer
Thank you for your Leadership
You make a difference

FAITHFUL
LIFE
PUBLISHERS & PRINTERS

Get to the Point
Copyright © 2017 by Gregory Ford

Hard cover ISBN: 978-1-63073-208-0

Paperback ISBN: 978-1-63073-205-9

eBook ISBN: 978-1-63073-209-7

Faithful Life Publishers & Printers
North Fort Myers, FL 33903

FaithfulLifePublishers.com
info@FaithfulLifePublishers.com
888.720.0950

The writings and teachings of this publication are presented by the author and do not necessarily reflect or represent the views, beliefs or opinions held by Faithful Life Publishers.

20 19 18 17   1 2 3 4 5

Table of Contents

Introduction

Get to the Point is a book that deals with turning points, paradigm shifts and God's divine transportation. It's about taking setbacks and turning them into comebacks. It's about God taking something that went wrong and turning it into a life-changing experience of empowerment, wisdom and knowledge. It's the classroom of purpose, process, evaluation and elevation. It's the revelation that anything worth having or doing comes with a cost. If something is of value and is a precious commodity, it doesn't come cheap.

First of all, what is a turning point? One definition is a time at which a decisive change in a situation occurs, especially one with beneficial results. Another definition is a point at which something changes direction or a moment when the course of events is changed. It's a critical point or a crisis. Another definition Is an event marking a unique or historical change of course. In life, sometimes your own personal definitions are the most significant, because turning points manifest in multiple ways, seasons and cycles of our lives. We all see and understand our turning points differently, because we all see life through a different set of lenses. Your turning point could be a death, loss or change in career opportunities. It could be a series of catastrophic events that somehow bring about an awakening, like what the Prodigal Son experienced when he came to his senses in Luke 15. This book will take you through many different kinds of possible turning points and paradigm shifts, helping to explore God's hand at work through the many seasons of life.

Most of us have experienced seasons of transitional activity, and after the settling of the winds and rains of chaos and frustration, we realize that the disruption was designed to either throw us off course or position us for destiny. Many names have been given to these situations: paradigm shifts, rude awakenings, shake-ups and others, but no matter what they have been called in the past, I like to call them Turning Points. Sometimes these disruptions are due to the actions and plots of our enemies, haters and agitators. Others see our potential and future purpose, but never encourage us to step up and embrace our career or divine assignments. We also fight battles against our own personal weaknesses and flaws, such as lackadaisical living, a lack of drive and focus. Sometimes we encounter setbacks as a result of our own inexperience and lack of knowledge; other times, it's our lack of commitment or lack of faith, inconsistency that tarnishes our track record. We want God to do something big in our lives, but He can't do it without our active cooperation.

6 But without faith it is impossible to please him: for he that cometh to God must believe that he is, and that he is a rewarder of them that diligently seek him. Hebrews 11:6 (KJV)

You will see the above verse more than once in this study, because to truly master the challenges and setbacks of life, we must have the faith to perceive God's truth and plan in the spiritual realm, regardless of the obstacles we see around us in the natural world. It's life by divine design. It's moving closer and closer each day to the expected end.

Every individual has a chapter in life where they come to a personally pivotal place in their journey. As you turn the pages of this book, you will be confronted with personal questions and thoughts that challenge you to reflect and process your past, present and future activity. Hopefully, as you read these pages, you will find the answers to questions about how to cope with the positive and negative effects of life's turning points, how to overcome a bad turn, how the paradigm shifts and detours of life can become catalysts for change, how to live victoriously when life presents you with unfamiliar territory and how to find the strength to take a new road with God.

My mother, the late Nellie Ruth Chestnut (Ford), would always tell us as little boys, "That a man thinks he knows, he knows not the things that he ought to know." In other words, most situations contain hidden information and wisdom yet to be revealed about a situation, an individual or life encounter. My prayer is that this book will help you open your mind and heart to a greater outpouring of God's wisdom through every turn and season of your life.

Chapter 1

The First Turn:
Personal Weaknesses and Flaws

Have you ever been in the company of people who always have great ideas and plans to do things differently, ideas that are life-changing and encouraging, but never seem to get them done? They talk about their new strategies for exercise and weight loss, their new approaches to marriage and their surroundings, but never seem to get any of these plans off the ground. What about those financial new beginners, who have made bad decision after bad decision with their resources? They pledge to get help and counsel from financial advisors and take classes and seek programs to do better, but never seem to set the appointments or attend the classes and continue making the same mistakes. After hearing something over and over again that has the potential to ignite positive change, but instead is spoken out of the mouth of vanity and dry ambition, it becomes the same old, same old. It's just a conversation.

In their heads and hearts, these people perceive that they are engaging in a productive activity because they are discussing change and others are listening, but those who have watched these individuals' lives from a distance see that no forward motion has actually occurred. We are simply wasting time and energy if all we're going to do is talk about positive change but really have no true intention to follow through. It has been said that what you fail to confront, you cannot change. Nothing happens; nothing moves or is different until one gets up and does something about it. As in the story of "The Boy Who Cried Wolf," eventually the listeners grow weary of the constant promises of something that is never delivered. A conversation without activation is no manifestation of advancement and accomplishment.

The cause of this failure to launch is simple: It comes from personal weakness, from the flaws that have beset human beings since the fall of mankind in the Garden of Eden. Without concerted effort to change, these flaws become life-defining and can hold individuals back from attaining the victories God has in store for them.

A personal weakness is the thing that one finds hard to do, a defect or a place of continual failure. It manifests in multiple ways and dimensions such as never being pleased, irresponsibility, tardiness, moodiness, trifling, impatience, closed-mindedness, rudeness, and pessimism. Similarly, a flaw is defined as an unattractive or unsatisfactory feature, primarily in a person's character. These weaknesses and flaws are serious; however, there is hope. One must have a true desire for change and a new direction for their life.

Embrace the need for change.

> *13 No, dear brothers and sisters, I have not achieved it, but I focus on this one thing: Forgetting the past and looking forward to what lies ahead,* Philippians 3:13 (NLT)

> *13 Brethren, I count not myself to have apprehended: but this one thing I do, forgetting those things which are behind, and reaching forth unto those things which are before, 14 I press toward the mark for the prize of the high calling of God in Christ Jesus.* Philippians 3:13-14 (KJV)

Focus on the Goal.

> *12 I'm not saying that I have this all together, that I have it made. But I am well on my way, reaching out for Christ, who has so wondrously reached out for me. 13 Friends, don't get me wrong: By no means do I count myself an expert in all of this, but I've got my eye on the goal, where God is beckoning us onward—to Jesus. 14 I'm off and running, and I'm not turning back.* Philippians 3:12-14 (MSG)

Own up to Weaknesses and Faults.

> *16 Confess your faults one to another, and pray one for another, that ye may be healed. The effectual fervent prayer of a righteous man availeth much.* James 5:16 (KJV)

Believe that all things are possible.

> *26 But Jesus beheld them, and said unto them, with men this is impossible; but with God all things are possible.* Matthew 19:26 (KJV)

We can change and make a difference if we choose to believe!

A sermon preached many years ago spoke of the transforming power of God displayed in a story about Sid the Caterpillar. For many years, Sid was a crawling creature that would slide upon the earth from place to place. His perspective was always from a low and limited place. He couldn't see much or do much.

One day, Sid did the unexpected, made his way up a tree and positioned himself to be a part of a metamorphic experience that would change everything in his life. Somehow, Sid knew that his season of change had come and that for it to happen, he needed to make his move to higher ground.

Sid positioned himself upon the limbs of the trees, and a cocoon formed around him as a protective covering, like the ark that protected Noah, the animals and his family until the divine assignment of the Lord was accomplished. Inside of the cocoon, a supernatural work was taking shape, and what was formerly a caterpillar was now being transformed into a butterfly. After a period of time, what had held the worm in place could not hold him anymore, and the outer shell of Sid's cocoon cracked and continued to crack, until out came a new creature: a butterfly with wings to fly.

One cannot become a butterfly and remain a caterpillar.

The journey from caterpillar to butterfly is an intentional one, a process of putting ourselves into the right place for change, a place that is inhabited by other people on the same upward journey, rather than those who pull us down and keep us mired in failure and self-doubt. To become stronger, we must embrace the company of those who lift us up and bolster our faith, the right people to help us on our way.

33 Do not be misled: Bad company corrupts good character.
I Corinthians 15:33 (NIV)

33 Do not be deceived: Bad company ruins good morals.
I Corinthians 15:33 (ESV)

33 Be not deceived: evil communications corrupt good manners. I Corinthians 15:33(KJV)

33 Stop being deceived: Wicked friends lead to evil ends.
I Corinthians 15:33 (ISV)

Motivators and encouragers.

11 Wherefore comfort yourselves together, and edify one another, even as also ye do. I Thessalonians 5:11 (KJV)

11 Therefore encourage (admonish, exhort) one another and edify (strengthen and build up) one another, just as you are doing. I Thessalonians 5:11 (AMP)

9-11 God didn't set us up for an angry rejection but for salvation by our Master, Jesus Christ. He died for us, a death that triggered life. Whether we're awake with the living or asleep with the dead, we're alive with him! So speak encouraging words to one another. Build up hope so you'll all be together in this, no one left out, no one left behind. I know you're already doing this; just keep on doing it. 1 Thessalonians 5:9-11 (MSG)

36 And Joses, who by the apostles was surnamed Barnabas, (which is, being interpreted, the son of consolation,) a Levite, and of the country of Cyprus, Acts 4:36 (KJV)

36 now Joseph, a Levite and native of Cyprus who was surnamed Barnabas by the apostles, which interpreted means Son of Encouragement, Acts 4:36 (AMP)

36 And so it was that Joseph, a Levite born in Cyprus, whom the apostles called Barnabas (which means 'One who Encourages'), Acts 4:36 (GNT)

36-37 Joseph, called by the apostles 'Barnabas' (which means 'Son of Comfort'), a Levite born in Cyprus, sold a field that he owned, brought the money, and made an offering of it to the apostles. Acts 4:36-37 (MSG)

29 But Jesus looked at them and said, 'With people [as far as it depends on them] it is impossible, but with God all things are possible. Matthew 19:26 (AMP)

29 Yeshua looked at them and said, 'Humanly, this is impossible; but with God everything is possible.' Matthew 19:26 (CJB)

29 Jesus looked straight at them and said, 'There are some things that people cannot do, but God can do anything.' Matthew 19:26 (CEV)

Those who hold us accountable.

17 Iron sharpeneth iron; so a man sharpeneth the countenance of his friend. Proverbs 27:17 (KJV)

1 Brethren, if a man be overtaken in a fault, ye which are spiritual, restore such a one in the spirit of meekness; considering thyself, lest thou also be tempted. 2 Bear ye one another's burdens, and so fulfill the law of Christ. Galatians 6:1-2 (KJV)

9 Two are better than one; because they have a good reward for their labour. 10 For if they fall, the one will lift up his fellow: but woe to him that is alone when he falleth; for he hath not another to help him up. 11 Again, if two lie together, then they have heat: but how can one be warm alone? 12 And if one prevail against him, two shall withstand him; and a threefold cord is not quickly broken. Ecclesiastes 4:9-12 (KJV)

Those who propel us toward righteous living.

24 And let us consider how we may spur one another on toward love and good deeds, Hebrews 10:24 (NIV)

24 Let us help each other to love others and to do good. Hebrews 10:24 (NLV)

Hebrew 11:6 says, *But without faith it is impossible to please him: for he that cometh to God must believe that he is, and that he is a rewarder of them that diligently seek him.* (KJV)

You have to believe in God and in yourself to become a victor in the battle against personal weaknesses and flaws. For many who are fighting this battle, your greatest struggle is your inner self, convincing *you* that *you can do this*. It's like preaching your first revival; it's overcoming the enemies in your own house. You must be all in and take ownership of the situation by demanding of yourself that you follow through. Upgrading has to be your personal goal.

Next, you must pursue overcoming your past by turning the negatives into positives and sticking with it until you see what you're seeking after. You must be diligent and remain focused. I heard a definition some time ago that is accurate and fitting: "Diligence is doing a small thing for a long time, until something big happens." *Stick with it!* Many people in ministries around the world want God to do something significant, powerful and impacting, but what we want God to do cannot be done without our involvement.

Ask yourself: How badly do you want change, new development and new life?

46 And they came to Jericho: and as he went out of Jericho with his disciples and a great number of people, blind Bartimaeus, the son of Timaeus, sat by the highway side begging.

47 And when he heard that it was Jesus of Nazareth, he began to cry out, and say, Jesus, thou son of David, have mercy on me.

48 And many charged him that he should hold his peace: but he cried the more a great deal, Thou son of David, have mercy on me.

49 And Jesus stood still, and commanded him to be called. And they call the blind man, saying unto him, Be of good comfort, rise; he calleth thee.

50 And he, casting away his garment, rose, and came to Jesus.

51 And Jesus answered and said unto him, What wilt thou that I should do unto thee? The blind man said unto him, Lord, that I might receive my sight.

52 And Jesus said unto him, Go thy way; thy faith hath made thee whole. And immediately he received his sight, and followed Jesus in the way. Mark 10:46-52 (KJV)

Exceptional Faith.

The blind man: he heard, he desired and he pursued his life-changing moment by getting up and doing something about it. ***He stuck with it!*** Even when others didn't agree or support his endeavors for change, he refused to be denied opportunity. His relentless pursuit of a miraculous metamorphosis came with a cost, and he was willing to pay the price. His exceptional faith positioned him to seize the moment and accomplish the impossible.

You can do better and be better, but the cost is not cheap. To pursue physical wholeness, the blind man had to brave human disapproval and go far outside his comfort zone. We must do the same if we are ever to achieve wholeness in our areas of weakness. If you want to change your inconsistencies, your personal weaknesses and the flaws in your life into positive and productive strengths, you have to seek God's help, wisdom and guidance, along with the counsel and advice of those who have been where you're going.

For man's extremity is God's opportunity!

Questions for Contemplation

1. What is one change you desire to see happen in your life?

_____

_____

_____

_____

2. Name a weakness that has held you back from reaching this change in the past.

_____

_____

_____

_____

3. When you think about Sid the Caterpillar, where do you see yourself? Are you still a caterpillar going along as usual, are you moving to a place of change, or have you entered the chrysalis of change? Are you ready to move to the next stage? Why or why not?

_____

_____

_____

4. Are you attracted to people who have a positive, forward-thinking outlook, or do you gravitate toward those who pull you back to the status quo? What about you? Are you a lifter or a discourager?

_____

_____

_____

_____

5. The blind man had to leave his comfort zone to reach wholeness. How might God be asking you to abandon your comfort zone today?

_____

_____

_____

_____

Chapter 2

The Second Turn: The Battle of the Lack of Knowledge and Experience

Have you ever encountered a moment in life when people responded to you in this manner: "Sorry, sir or ma'am, I am afraid you don't meet the qualifications to be employed on this job?" That is one of the most disappointing and discouraging things a person can ever hear.

What about the statement that says you're overqualified? Really? What is "overqualified?" I would like to think that if I was overqualified, that I not only have what it takes to do the job, but have additional insight and expertise that would be beneficial to the company. Whatever the reason given, being told that an opportunity is just out of reach because you do not have the right things to offer is daunting and deeply frustrating.

What about the times when someone says, "It's not your time yet," or, "Just be patient?" Compliments about your gifts and talents, even assurances that you will be a blessing somewhere else, ring hollow when they come on the heels of a denial of your fitness for something you believe is your perfect opportunity.

So-called comforting words are often unleashed, statements that involve Scripture, in order to keep us from a major letdown.

People quote verses about waiting on the Lord, and they expect us to cheerfully agree with them. More often than not, we feel that pressure and tell them they must be right, so these supposed comforters go on to say, "Wait it out. Surely you're the next one to get the promotion or position." Somehow, though, our moment never seems to arrive, no matter how long we wait.

How many times have we heard these statements being said to us or someone close to us? For various reasons and on many occasions, we have all heard them said to those in our circles of influence or spoken to us directly. Whether they are words of "not enough," "too much," or "not yet," they simply sound like disappointment and deferred hope when they hit our ears and the ears of those we love.

In his poem Harlem, poet Langston Hughes asked the famous question, "What happens to a dream deferred?" When does the change come, we ask? When will things shift and begin to work in my favor? Waiting passively simply isn't enough. As many have said, the definition of insanity is doing the same thing over and over and expecting a different result.

11 What strength do I have, that I should still hope? What prospects, that I should be patient? Job 6:11 (NIV)

The change that we are seeking is already within us, a seed God has planted that He wants to nurture to full maturity.

13 for it is God who works in you to will and to act in order to fulfill his good purpose. Philippians 2:13 (NIV)

26-27 Take a good look, friends, at who you were when you got called into this life. I don't see many of 'the brightest and the best' among you, not many influential, not many from high-

society families. Isn't it obvious that God deliberately chose men and women that the culture overlooks and exploits and abuses, chose these 'nobodies' to expose the hollow pretensions of the 'somebodies'? 1 Corinthians 1:26-27 (MSG)

Seeds do not grow overnight, and just because something has the potential to grow up strong and vibrant does not mean that it will automatically do so. If you go to the nursery, purchase a plant for your garden, and bring it home, do you set it somewhere and hope for the best? No, you bring home instructions for how to care for your new acquisition, and you carefully follow those instructions to nurture it to maturity, knowing that if you leave it alone, nothing will happen but decay.

Our lives, like the plants in a garden, will not grow and blossom without specific, targeted effort. If we do not make the choice to go forward, working with faith, we will see decay in ourselves and our opportunities.

We are mistaken if we think we can continue on as we always have and simply wait for change to come. Change is not a passive thing that happens to us. It is a prize that we seize with the help of God's Spirit within us, empowering and strengthening our efforts.

12 Therefore, my beloved, as you have always obeyed, so now, not only as in my presence but much more in my absence, work out your own salvation with fear and trembling, 13 for it is God who works in you, both to will and to work for his good pleasure. Philippians 2:12-13 (ESV)

If you want something that you have never had, you will have to do something you have never done. The difference-maker is you! Everything you need to move forward and advance toward your change for the better is already in you. It needs to be brought up from within, so that your purpose and potential will be seen and no longer denied.

> *11 And God said, Let the earth bring forth grass, the herb yielding seed, and the fruit tree yielding fruit after his kind, whose seed is in itself, upon the earth: and it was so. 12 And the earth brought forth grass, and herb yielding seed after his kind, and the tree yielding fruit, whose seed was in itself, after his kind: and God saw that it was good.* Genesis 1:11-12 (KJV)

> *13 I can do all things through Christ which strengtheneth me.* Philippians 4:13 (KJV)

The bottom line here is the question we must ask ourselves: Did I do my full part to prepare for this moment of opportunity? We can find many circumstances and other people to blame, but when it comes down to it, we need to look in the mirror and recognize our own responsibility.

Have you ever left an appointment, test, or interview thinking, "I could have done better?" Have you recognized the real problem, that maybe you've **played** more than you've **paid**? Do you ever consider the possibility that you've lost focus and forgotten that the next level and promotion in life will come with a cost?

> *11 We hear that some among you are idle and disruptive. They are not busy; they are busybodies. 12 Such people we command and urge in the Lord Jesus Christ to settle down and earn the food they eat. 13 And as for you, brothers and sisters, never tire of doing what is good.* 2 Thessalonians 3:11-13 (NIV)

> *4 A slack hand causes poverty, but the hand of the diligent makes rich.* Proverbs 10:4 (ESV)

5 The plans of the diligent lead surely to abundance and advantage, But everyone who acts in haste comes surely to poverty. Proverbs 21:5 (AMP)

Your downtime is the most important resource you possess. What are you doing while you wait for your opportunity? No great endeavor that we attempt will ever come cheap; there are no automatic gains on the journey to success. Anything we achieve comes from God-anointed determination, effort, and diligence.

11 We want each of you to show this same diligence to the very end, so that what you hope for may be fully realized. Hebrews 6:11 (NIV)

23 Whatever you do, work at it with all your heart, as working for the Lord, not for human masters, 24 since you know that you will receive an inheritance from the Lord as a reward. It is the Lord Christ you are serving. Colossians 3:23-24 (NIV)

We must examine ourselves often and ask the question: "Have I truly done what it takes to bring my desire to fruition?" Perhaps this time in your life will require a stronger work ethic and a new level of creativity. To change your circumstances, you must first change your outlook.

What worked in one season of your life will not get it done in this season. You cannot continue to do exactly the same things and expect different results to magically appear. Changing your outlook and behavior are necessary parts of changing your circumstances and achieving your dreams.

3 Commit your work to the Lord, and your plans will be established. Proverbs 16:3 (ESV)

Change begets change.

9 Let us not lose heart in doing good, for in due time we will reap if we do not grow weary. Galatians 6:9 (NASB)

The good news is that we do not serve a God of sameness and mediocrity. Instead, we serve an infinitely creative God, who longs to help us reach new heights of opportunity and success. Just as He is not a passive observer of our lives, we, as bearers of His image, are called to be active participants in our lives and our world. Only as we choose to step up in conjunction with Him will we begin to see our change occurring.

16 A man's gift makes room for him and brings him before the great. Proverbs 18:16 (ESV)

In order to progress, we must be willing to do what is necessary to work with Him to take our lives to the next level He has in store for us. Doing the same things the same way will not cut it any more. We must take hold of God's promises and the gifts He has placed within us and begin ***moving forward*** toward the prize He has in store.

19 See, I am doing a new thing! Now it springs up; do you not perceive it? I am making a way in the wilderness and streams in the wasteland. Isaiah 43:19 (NIV)

17 Therefore if anyone is in Christ, he is a new creature; the old things passed away; behold, new things have come. 2 Corinthians 5:17 (NASB)

Change is on the horizon! To receive it, we must be willing to cooperate actively with the One who desires us to flourish even more than we do. In God's hands, every seed of our potential can grow to become a fully-realized asset in our lives.

> *11 For I know the plans I have for you, declares the Lord, plans for welfare and not for evil, to give you a future and a hope.* Jeremiah 29:11 (ESV)

> *2 Enlarge the place of your tent, and let the curtains of your habitations be stretched out; do not hold back; lengthen your cords and strengthen your stakes.* Isaiah 54:2 (ESV)

> *7 But as for you, be strong and do not give up, for your work will be rewarded.* 2 Chronicles 15:7 (NIV)

Questions for Contemplation

1. Think of a time in your life when you reached for a new opportunity, only to be turned down. How did you feel? What did you do in response?

_____

_____

_____

_____

2. Do you really believe that the potential for change is already inside you, or do you struggle to grasp this truth? Why or why not?

_____

_____

_____

_____

_____

3. What is one change you've made in the past that led to positive results later on? Did those results make your effort feel more worthwhile?

_____

_____

_____

_____

4. What obstacles in your life are keeping you chained to sameness and passivity?

_____

_____

_____

_____

5. What is one dream you hold right now that has yet to be fully realized?

_____

_____

_____

_____

Chapter 3

The Third Turn: Overcoming the Fear of Change

Do it differently this time!

On the surface, that sounds like simple enough advice, but those of us who are alive and breathing know that it really isn't, don't we? Even when we've worked to gain the knowledge and experience we need to succeed, we can still be held back by our own fear of doing what we have perceived, in the past, to be difficult, even impossible. The irony is that our fear of not succeeding can lead us to never even try, which means automatic failure! Any change we're too afraid to reach toward is a change we will never achieve.

The good news is that fear doesn't have to hold us back from reaching our full, God-given potential! Even for those who struggle deeply with the fear of change and anxiety about leaving their comfort zone, God's promises provide hope beyond measure and the promise that this battle can be won!

> *10 So do not fear, for I am with you; do not be dismayed, for I am your God. I will strengthen you and help you; I will uphold you with my righteous right hand.* Isaiah 41:10 (NIV)

6 Do not be anxious about anything, but in every situation, by prayer and petition, with thanksgiving, present your requests to God. 7 And the peace of God, which transcends all understanding, will guard your hearts and your minds in Christ Jesus. Philippians 4:6-7 (NIV)

10 For we are His workmanship [His own master work, a work of art], created in Christ Jesus [reborn from above— spiritually transformed, renewed, ready to be used] for good works, which God prepared [for us] beforehand [taking paths which He set], so that we would walk in them [living the good life which He prearranged and made ready for us]. Ephesians 2:10 (AMP)

The Bible offers many examples of individuals choosing courageous behavior in spite of their fear, but the second chapter of Mark presents a unique example of four men who chose faith over fear in the face of seemingly-insurmountable obstacles. Let's read their story:

The Man of Palsy

3 And they come unto him, bringing one sick of the palsy, which was borne of four. 4 And when they could not come nigh unto him for the press, they uncovered the roof where he was: and when they had broken it up, they let down the bed wherein the sick of the palsy lay. Mark 2:3-4 (KJV)

Sit back and take a close look at this scene, These men who brought their friend to Jesus were undoubtedly extremely tired from the journey of carrying him down the rocky and dusty road leading into Capernaum. They bore him, they carried him, and they labored in love.

17 A friend loves at all times, and a brother is born for a time of adversity. Proverbs 17:17 (NIV)

The friendship and loyalty of these men showed true commitment to helping their friend achieve change. Even to get him to the house required a boldness and a refusal to bow to the fear of how complicated it must have been to get a severely injured man to the house.

7 Be strong and very courageous. Be careful to obey all the law my servant Moses gave you; do not turn from it to the right or to the left, that you may be successful wherever you go. Joshua 1:7 (NIV)

What we see in Scripture is a display of tremendous sacrifice, and, often, change in our lives requires tremendous sacrifice as well. Even though fear is not an enjoyable thing, holding onto our fear can become a crutch for us. Letting go of what we're used to can seem unthinkable.

Faith is what enables us to believe the sacrifice will prove to be worth it.

2 And walk in the way of love, just as Christ loved us and gave himself up for us as a fragrant offering and sacrifice to God. Ephesians 5:2 (NIV)

24 For whoever wishes to save his life will lose it, but whoever loses his life for My sake, he is the one who will save it. Luke 9:24 (NASB)

8 More than that, I also consider everything to be a loss in view of the surpassing value of knowing Christ Jesus my Lord. Because of Him I have suffered the loss of all things and consider them filth, so that I may gain Christ. Philippians 3:8 (HCSB)

These friends heard that Jesus was in a nearby home in the city, and they knew that the power to heal their friend was nigh. They believed, as we are also called to believe, that Jesus could change their friend's life with His miraculous healing power.

After finally arriving at the location and seeing the crowd of people gathered around the house, they searched diligently for an entrance into the presence of Jesus, but found none; however, they had come too far; they had been through too much to turn back in defeat. In our own lives, we must make this same determination. We have come too far to turn back before our change is complete, and God calls us ever forward, in spite of the obstacles we face.

> *9 Let us not become weary in doing good, for at the proper time we will reap a harvest if we do not give up.* Galatians 6:9 (NIV)

When the path to change seems blocked and arduous, don't change your mind about your God-given goals; change your strategy!

A time comes in your life when failure is not an option, no matter how apprehensive you may feel. These men flatly refused to go home with their friend in the same state they had brought him in. I can imagine them saying to one another, "There has to be another way in!" Despite the fear they must have felt, they refused to give up on their God-given mission.

Surely there's a way in for us as well, but it will require moving beyond the familiar mindset of taking the usual way in *so that we can find an untapped entrance to obtain uncommon access.* These friends came up with a new plan that spoke of their courageous and bold character. This is how Jesus responded to their faith:

11 I say unto thee, Arise, and take up thy bed, and go thy way into thine house. 12 And immediately he arose, took up the bed, and went forth before them all; insomuch that they were all amazed, and glorified God, saying, We never saw it on this fashion. Mark 2:11-12 (KJV)

The extraordinary effort of four friends brought the man to Jesus, who healed him and altered his life forever. Their boldness to do what had never been done made way for a change that would not have happened if they had shrunk back in fear from the difficulty of accomplishing the task before them.

9 Have I not commanded you? Be strong and courageous. Do not be terrified; do not be discouraged, for the Lord your God will be with you wherever you go. Joshua 1:9 (NIV)

What are you willing to do to overcome the obstacles and issues that deny you access to what you came for? These men were boldly willing to do the uncommon to take their friend into the presence of the Lord. All apparent entrances were closed: the courtyards, doorways and windows were full, but because of true friends who had the kind of faith that would not settle for defeat, the roof was the next assignment. With bold faith, they broke it up and lowered him down into the presence of Jesus. What about your breakthrough?

Are you willing to stand against the fear and anxiety that circumstances and obstacles bring, in order to achieve the change you seek?

7 For God gave us a spirit not of fear but of power and love and self-control. 2 Timothy 1:7 (ESV)

These friends did what they had to do to get what their disabled companion had never had. In the same situation, most would have probably turned back, too timid and scared of the consequences to make the attempt. Instead, these unnamed men are an example of the kind of boldness that gets things done, the God-given power to stand against common obstacles to achieve unusual dreams. The same God who gave them the strength to stand against fear and apprehension is ready and willing to help us conquer these same obstacles today!

> *27 Peace I leave with you; my peace I give you. I do not give to you as the world gives. Do not let your hearts be troubled and do not be afraid.* John 14:27 (NIV)

> *4 Little children, you are from God and have overcome them, for he who is in you is greater than he who is in the world.* 1 John 4:4 (ESV)

> *19 Behold, I have given you authority to tread on serpents and scorpions, and over all the power of the enemy, and nothing shall hurt you. 20 Nevertheless, do not rejoice in this, that the spirits are subject to you, but rejoice that your names are written in heaven.* Luke 10:19-20 (ESV)

> *11 Behold, all who are incensed against you shall be put to shame and confounded; those who strive against you shall be as nothing and shall perish. 12 You shall seek those who contend with you, but you shall not find them; those who war against you shall be as nothing at all. 13 For I, the Lord your God, hold your right hand; it is I who say to you, Fear not, I am the one who helps you.'* Isaiah 41:11-13 (ESV)

Questions for Contemplation

1. What is something in your life that makes you comfortable? How does it benefit you? How might it be holding you back?

_____

_____

_____

_____

2. Recall a time in your life when a friend's faith helped you reach your goal.

_____

_____

_____

3. Now recall a time when your faith helped a friend achieve their goal. What did you learn from that experience?

_____

_____

_____

_____

4. What goal do you have that you lack courage to achieve? (Be honest.)

_____

_____

_____

_____

5. Pick one of the victorious verses from this chapter and write it out by hand. While you do so, pray that verse in faith for your situation.

_____

_____

_____

_____

Chapter 4

The Fourth Turn: Finding the Right Mentors

The way to excel at this turn is to surround yourself with people who have the ability to do the following three things in your life: They must be able to **prep**, **shape** and **condition** you for your future. Any good athlete seeks out an excellent coach and trainer, because without the right kind of mentorship, no person can reach their fullest potential.

I am presently sitting in my office watching previews of the NBA finals, and I can easily see that for either of these teams to have made it this far on this long season's journey, they must have had a system in place that prepared and conditioned the athletes. Without a doubt, they had trainers who spent countless hours working with the players to keep them physically ready.

So, I ask you, who is mentoring you? Corporate giants, athletes, the very elite persons who have reached major points of success, all have one thing in common: They had people around them—mentors, life coaches, or spiritual leaders—who helped them attain success. Understand that no man is an island unto himself, and no one will make it to the top alone.

Consider 1 Kings 17:1-24 (KJV)

1 And Elijah the Tishbite, who was of the inhabitants of Gilead, said unto Ahab, As the Lord God of Israel liveth, before whom I stand, there shall not be dew nor rain these years, but according to my word.

2 And the word of the Lord came unto him, saying,

3 Get thee hence, and turn thee eastward, and hide thyself by the brook Cherith that is before Jordan.

4 And it shall be, that thou shalt drink of the brook; and I have commanded the ravens to feed thee there.

5 So he went and did according unto the word of the Lord: for he went and dwelt by the brook Cherith, that is before Jordan.

6 And the ravens brought him bread and flesh in the morning, and bread and flesh in the evening; and he drank of the brook.

7 And it came to pass after a while, that the brook dried up, because there had been no rain in the land.

8 And the word of the Lord came unto him, saying,

9 Arise, get thee to Zarephath, which belongeth to Zidon, and dwell there: behold, I have commanded a widow woman there to sustain thee.

10 So he arose and went to Zarephath. And when he came to the gate of the city, behold, the widow woman was there gathering of sticks: and he called to her, and said, Fetch me, I pray thee, a little water in a vessel, that I may drink.

11 And as she was going to fetch it, he called to her, and said, Bring me, I pray thee, a morsel of bread in thine hand.

12 And she said, As the Lord thy God liveth, I have not a cake, but an handful of meal in a barrel, and a little oil in a cruse: and, behold, I am gathering two sticks, that I may go in and dress it for me and my son, that we may eat it, and die.

13 And Elijah said unto her, Fear not; go and do as thou hast said: but make me thereof a little cake first, and bring it unto me, and after make for thee and for thy son.

14 For thus saith the Lord God of Israel, The barrel of meal shall not waste, neither shall the cruse of oil fail, until the day that the Lord sendeth rain upon the earth.

15 And she went and did according to the saying of Elijah: and she, and he, and her house, did eat many days.

16 And the barrel of meal wasted not, neither did the cruse of oil fail, according to the word of the Lord, which he spake by Elijah.

17 And it came to pass after these things, that the son of the woman, the mistress of the house, fell sick; and his sickness was so sore, that there was no breath left in him.

18 And she said unto Elijah, What have I to do with thee, O thou man of God? art thou come unto me to call my sin to remembrance, and to slay my son?

19 And he said unto her, Give me thy son. And he took him out of her bosom, and carried him up into a loft, where he abode, and laid him upon his own bed.

20 And he cried unto the Lord, and said, O Lord my God, hast thou also brought evil upon the widow with whom I sojourn, by slaying her son?

21 And he stretched himself upon the child three times, and cried unto the Lord, and said, O Lord my God, I pray thee, let this child's soul come into him again.

22 And the Lord heard the voice of Elijah; and the soul of the child came into him again, and he revived.

23 And Elijah took the child, and brought him down out of the chamber into the house, and delivered him unto his mother: and Elijah said, See, thy son liveth.

24 And the woman said to Elijah, Now by this I know that thou art a man of God, and that the word of the Lord in thy mouth is truth.

The Prophet Elijah, whom we see being greatly used of God in this story, also struggled mightily after experiencing great success on Mount Carmel. He found himself hiding out in a cave, dealing with fear, depression and loneliness. God sent an angel to visit the prophet and say, *Elijah, come out of this cave.*

Even bold people of God need help to achieve their divinely-appointed purposes and escape from the traps of failure and discouragement. The man who, through the power of God, was able to call the dead back to life, was not beyond needing help, and neither are you and I.

Somebody somewhere is equipped with what you need to live out your purpose. Your job is to pray that God brings you to them or directs them to you. You must sit with those who have been where you want to go and have already made it. Listen up, suit up and walk up. In time, you may find that the Lord calls you to be someone else's mentor, just as Elijah was appointed to mentor Elisha and ready him for ministry.

5 The wise will hear and increase their learning, And the person of understanding will acquire wise counsel and the skill [to steer his course wisely and lead others to the truth]
Proverbs 1:5 (AMP)

At times, you need people in your life who can save you from failing a test you should be able to pass. God will divinely place people in your path from whose experiences you are able to glean and learn wisdom, those who will cause you to excel and not linger in certain seasons longer than God originally intended. Those are the ones I like to call the "been there, done that, spent the night and got a t-shirt" people. They are those who survived it and can share with you the pitfalls, the do's and don'ts.

Along this way to accomplishing purpose and fulfillment are many distractions. When you're pursuing life-changing opportunities, good mentors will help you stay the course until the mission is accomplished.

> *7 Remember your leaders, those who spoke to you the word of God. Consider the outcome of their way of life, and imitate their faith.* Hebrews 13:7 (ESV)

If you know that you need something, go and get it! God is telling you through your circumstances that you can be better, wiser and stronger; however, achievement comes with a cost. Don't fear learning from someone who has made it through and exited on the other side. A wise man once said, "Learning something may take you a lifetime, but learning what you did will take me a lunch time."

You have to be willing to hit the gym, go to the library and the classroom. You have to have people in your life who prep, shape and condition you for the call or assignment upon your life, and you must be willing to follow their instructions. These are people who will stretch, push, and pull you in the direction of your destiny. These are people who are determined to see you reach the finish line. They are not always your cheerleader, but they are the ones who always have your best interest at in mind. Dreams do come true, but if God is going to do anything through your life, He cannot do it without your active cooperation. He needs your participation.

Even after spending more than twenty-five years in ministry, preaching and teaching the gospel to thousands, I had to desire an upgrade of my own and have a drive to pursue the goal of higher education in biblical studies. Without the willingness to do what it took, I could not have achieved the change I wanted to see. I started out with small steps. I enrolled in a biblical studies course while I was still pastoring, preaching, evangelizing and completing all the duties that go along with my role as a spiritual leader.

I was already a husband, a father and a community leader, but I still wanted more. I acquired my Associates Degree in Theology, but I did not stop there. In three years, I had my Bachelor of Arts Degree in Theology, and later I became an ordained minister of the Assemblies of God. The change started with a desire in my heart to pursue more knowledge and understanding about God and a deeper understanding of His Word, but along the way I had to be willing to cooperate with the mentorship of God and with the human teachers and mentors He placed along my path to success.

Good mentors help you pursue knowledge and find your own personal upgrade. Knowledge is power, and the more you know about a thing the better you are going to be at it.

15 Study to shew thyself approved unto God. 2 Timothy 2:15a (KJV)

Study what it takes to become who you desire to be, and then pursue whatever it takes to stay on top. Set your mind on progressively growing and not declining, letting the challenges of your mentors propel you forward instead of intimidating you.

You have to find out what it takes to become better. You must ask, what do I have to know and go through to get to the next level. What is my journey from where I am now to fulfillment? When people see you reaching for your God-given purpose, they will make investments in you by reminding you of what it takes to become what you dream.

Diligence, discipline, hard work and continual study are vital elements you must pursue in order to be ready when your season of visitation and promotion come, and godly mentors will enable you to know how to direct your efforts in the best way possible.

If you combine your efforts with the wisdom of godly mentors, you won't be caught short in the end. You will be fully prepared when your opportunities come.

Questions for Contemplation

1. Recall a time when you faced a challenge you were unprepared to meet. What might you have done to change the outcome?

_____

_____

_____

_____

2. Now, recall a challenge you succeeded in meeting. What did you do differently that time?

_____

_____

_____

_____

3. Does it surprise you that a powerful man of God like Elijah needed help to escape from his web of discouragement and accomplish God's purpose for him? Why or why not?

_____

_____

_____

_____

4. How have mentors helped you in the past? (Remember, a mentor can go by the name of coach, teacher, pastor or other leader.)

_____

_____

_____

_____

5. List an area (or areas) in which you currently need guidance to get you to the next level. Are you willing to take the faith step of asking someone to help you achieve your goal?

_____

_____

_____

_____

Chapter 5

The Fifth Turn: Overcoming A Bad Turn

Thus far in this study, we've focused on positive opportunities on the road of life and how to navigate those turns in victory and anointing. The truth is, however, that every one of us will, at some point in our lives, make a bad turn. Wrong turns have been built into our human DNA since the fall of mankind.

We can be hobbled by toxic relationships, poor decisions, addictions, insecurities and the list goes on. Satan is creative, and he uses anything he can get his hands on in our lives to take us as far off God's road of faith and victory as he can.

We can also take a wrong turn entirely by accident. What seemed like a wonderful opportunity can turn out to be something other than what we expected. A choice can seem good to us but still be less than God's best. When a direction you wanted to go is suddenly blocked or you're divinely thwarted in your plans, thank God for His interventions, when He decides that it is your season for a turn around.

> *5 Trust in the Lord with all your heart, and do not lean on your own understanding. 6 In all your ways acknowledge him, and he will make straight your paths.* Proverbs 3:5-6 (ESV)

The battle against wrong turns is a very powerful battle, and if we do not win, we are doomed. The wonderful news is that no wrong turn we're facing, whether we took it yesterday or twenty years ago, is terminal. We have a God who is ready and waiting to help us win this battle if we will simply stop on whatever road we're currently taking and ask Him for directions back to His divinely-appointed pathway.

The first step we must take is to realize and acknowledge that we've taken a wrong turn. This requires the humility to admit, before God and often before other people, that we're not perfect.

> *13 He who conceals his transgressions will not prosper, But whoever confesses and turns away from his sins will find compassion and mercy.* Proverbs 28:13 (AMP)

> *18 Pride goes before destruction, a haughty spirit before a fall.* Proverbs 16:18 (NIV)

Next, we must have real willingness to change. Merely admitting that something is wrong is only the first step toward fixing the problem. It's possible to acknowledge a wrong turn and then sit in it, wallowing in failure and mistakes until it becomes a way of life. We must repent, meaning that we change our mind and the way we think about the direction we're heading. We have to decide to head in a new direction, no matter how tempted we are to stay in our failed rut.

> *17 The highway of the upright is to depart from evil; He who keeps his way preserves his soul.* Proverbs 16:17 (NKJV)

> *7 For as he thinks in his heart, so is he.* Proverbs 23:7a (NKJV)

> *13 Brethren, I count not myself to have apprehended: but this one thing I do, forgetting those things which are behind, and*

reaching forth unto those things which are before, Philippians 3:13 (KJV)

Once we have acknowledged our mistake and determined to change, we are ready to unleash God's transforming power in our lives. If we ask for His help, God will not leave us where we are. Instead, He has promised to lead us back to the pathway of wholeness and fulfillment.

23 The Lord makes firm the steps of the one who delights in him; 24 though he may stumble, he will not fall, for the Lord upholds him with his hand. Psalm 37:23-24 (NIV)

32 It is God who arms me with strength and keeps my way secure. 33 He makes my feet like the feet of a deer; he causes me to stand on the heights. Psalm 18:32-33 (NIV)

A thrilling, supernatural mystery of Christian living is God's promise that everything in our lives works together for our good when we live according to His plan. Once we allow Him to lead us back to His pathway of success, He will take the wrong turns we've made and use them for His glory and our benefit, perhaps even for the benefit of others.

Maybe you'll be a "been there, done that" person some day, able to warn others about wrong turns. Perhaps you'll be an encourager, reminding others that no matter how far off course they've gone, your life proves that God's grace is sufficient for restoration. None of us can predict the ministry God has in store for us once we are back on His pathway, but the point is that nothing in His kingdom is wasted. Consecrated to Him, even your wrong turns will transform into assets.

28 And we know that all things work together for good to them that love God, to them who are the called according to his purpose. Romans 8:28 (KJV)

Consider the life of the Apostle Paul, the one who penned Philippians 3 under divine inspiration, powerfully declaring his intention to forget the things behind him and press toward Christ's purposes in his life. He sounds like such a saint, doesn't he? Surely a man with such powerful, forward-looking faith never took a wrong turn.

You might think that, but you'd be incorrect. The life of Paul, previously known as Saul, is described in Acts chapters 8-9:

3 But Saul was ravaging the church, and entering house after house, he dragged off men and women and committed them to prison. Acts 8:3 (ESV)

1 But Saul, still breathing threats and murder against the disciples of the Lord, went to the high priest 2 and asked him for letters to the synagogues at Damascus, so that if he found any belonging to the Way, men or women, he might bring them bound to Jerusalem. Acts 9:1-2 (ESV)

The apostle who wrote Philippians once took such a wrong turn that he ended up being a murderous persecutor of early Christians, killing and imprisoning those who professed Jesus as Lord, thinking he was somehow serving God even while he committed atrocities against God's people. It's difficult to imagine anyone being more off course and outside God's divine purpose than this man.

And yet, this is the same man who wrote much of the New Testament. How in the world did a man's life course correct enough to get him from one place to the other? No human being could ever make that radical of a change on his own.

Let's look at the divine encounter recorded in Acts 9:3-19 (ESV) that changed Saul's life permanently:

3 Now as he went on his way, he approached Damascus, and suddenly a light from heaven shone around him.

4 And falling to the ground, he heard a voice saying to him, 'Saul, Saul, why are you persecuting me?'

5 And he said, 'Who are you, Lord?' And he said, 'I am Jesus, whom you are persecuting.

6 But rise and enter the city, and you will be told what you are to do.'

7 The men who were traveling with him stood speechless, hearing the voice but seeing no one.

8 Saul rose from the ground, and although his eyes were opened, he saw nothing. So they led him by the hand and brought him into Damascus.

9 And for three days he was without sight, and neither ate nor drank.

10 Now there was a disciple at Damascus named Ananias. The Lord said to him in a vision, 'Ananias.' And he said, 'Here I am, Lord.'

11 And the Lord said to him, 'Rise and go to the street called Straight, and at the house of Judas look for a man of Tarsus named Saul, for behold, he is praying,

12 and he has seen in a vision a man named Ananias come in and lay his hands on him so that he might regain his sight.'

13 But Ananias answered, 'Lord, I have heard from many about this man, how much evil he has done to your saints at Jerusalem.

14 And here he has authority from the chief priests to bind all who call on your name.' 15 But the Lord said to him, 'Go, for he is a chosen instrument of mine to carry my name before the Gentiles and kings and the children of Israel.

16 For I will show him how much he must suffer for the sake of my name.'

17 So Ananias departed and entered the house. And laying his hands on him he said, 'Brother Saul, the Lord Jesus who appeared to you on the road by which you came has sent me so that you may regain your sight and be filled with the Holy Spirit.'

18 And immediately something like scales fell from his eyes, and he regained his sight. Then he rose and was baptized;

19 and taking food, he was strengthened.

Saul's encounter with God on the road to Damascus gave him the strength to turn permanently from his erroneous path and become the Apostle Paul. To overcome our own wrong turns, we also need to seek our own Damascus experience with God, an encounter in which we surrender our failings to Him and allow His divine strength to course correct our lives back to His perfect pathway.

As the Reverend V. Crandall Miller often said, "The Kingdom of God is a matter of direction, not distance." No matter how many mistakes we've made or how many wrong turns we've taken in the past, what matters is what direction we're heading **now**.

Victorious living isn't achieving an impossible standard of perfection. It's moving closer and closer each day to the expected end.

13 Brothers, I do not consider that I have made it my own. But one thing I do: forgetting what lies behind and straining forward to what lies ahead, 14 I press on toward the goal for the prize of the upward call of God in Christ Jesus. Philippians 3:13-14 (ESV)

Questions for Contemplation

1. Many people find it hard to ask for directions on the highway, let alone in life. Why do you think it's so difficult for human beings to admit that they've gone off course?

_____

_____

_____

_____

2. Think of a time in the past when you took a bad turn in your life. What happened?

_____

_____

_____

3. What stood out to you in our study of the life of the Apostle Paul?

_____

_____

_____

_____

4. What area(s) of your life is off course today?

_____

_____

_____

_____

5. Write out a prayer asking God to bring you to a Damascus encounter with His grace and power to get you back on course.

_____

_____

_____

_____

Chapter 6

The Sixth Turn: Seeing Beyond the Enemy

The biblical book of 2 Kings, chapter six, tells a story of the prophet Elisha. Through divine intervention, the prophet was made aware of the conversation of the King of Syria, who was talking about his plan to ambush the army of Israel. The Lord opened up the prophetic channels and airwaves to reveal the secrets of the king's heart, his discussion and strategy to overtake God's chosen people.

In the natural, Israel's forces had no way of learning what the Syrians planned to do, but God enabled the prophet to see beyond what was in front of him to learn what seemed to be hidden. Through Elisha, He gave His people the ability to see beyond the enemy's hold on their situation and to gain information that would give them the victory.

3 Call to me and I will answer you and tell you great and unsearchable things you do not know. Jeremiah 33:3 (NIV)

Elisha, who had received this information from God, gave the notice to the King of Israel that the enemy nation was planning an ambush to bring harm to his people. Now, the King of Syria, after discovering that his plot was no longer a secret, thought that someone inside his court was going outside and communicating the secrets of his bedchamber:

8 Then the king of Syria warred against Israel, and took counsel with his servants, saying, In such and such a place shall be my camp. 9 And the man of God sent unto the king of Israel, saying, Beware that thou pass not such a place; for thither the Syrians are come down. 10 And the king of Israel sent to the place which the man of God told him and warned him of, and saved himself there, not once nor twice. 2 Kings 6:8-10 (KJV)

The king assumed that one of his men had betrayed him. He only had eyes to see what was in front of him, in the natural world. Therefore, he summoned his advisors to come together to enquire about who this might be. After questioning one another, one of his captains said to the King of Syria that it was not one of his men; instead, he said, it was that prophet in Israel named Elisha who had revealed the plans of the King of Syria to the King of Israel.

Filled with anger and rage, the king's only thought was of capturing this one man who had power to hear the secrets of another man's heart. He sent forth his army to capture Elisha; his desire was to shut him down. It was made known to the king that Elisha was in a place called Dothan, and with full force and power, the Syrian army surrounded the city of Dothan to take hold of Elisha.

Now the scene moves to the house occupied by Elisha and his servant in Dothan. When the servant got up in the morning, he went outside, and he saw that the Syrian army had surrounded the city. His immediate, terrified response to Elisha was, *Alas, my master! How shall we do?*

Without hesitation, but with God-given confidence, Elisha replied and said, *Fear not: for they that be with us are more than they that be with them.* And Elisha prayed, and said, *Lord, I pray thee, open his eyes, that he may see.*

14 Therefore sent he thither horses, and chariots, and a great host: and they came by night, and compassed the city about. 15 And when the servant of the man of God was risen early, and gone forth, behold, an host compassed the city both with horses and chariots. And his servant said unto him, Alas, my master! how shall we do? 16 And he answered, Fear not: for they that be with us are more than they that be with them. 17 And Elisha prayed, and said, Lord, I pray thee, open his eyes, that he may see. And the Lord opened the eyes of the young man; and he saw: and, behold, the mountain was full of horses and chariots of fire round about Elisha.
2 Kings 6:14-17 (KJV)

After Elisha's prayer, the servant was able to see what his natural, earthly-focused eyes had missed. He had no reason to be anxious or afraid, because *the mountain was full of horses and chariots of fire.* God's armies had come to the aid of Elisha and his servant.

Many times in life, we find ourselves looking at and focusing on the enemy and his attacks more than on the presence, power and promises of God. What we choose to focus on looms larger and larger in our view, until God's presence seems like a tiny speck in our peripheral vision compared to the huge, seemingly-insurmountable problems we face.

This is the opposite of reality, but in the natural, it seems like we're seeing things for what they are. We trust our understanding, rather than in God's truth. Our gaze becomes so rooted in the natural that we fail to see the evidences of God's power all around us.

5 Trust in the Lord with all your heart, and do not lean on your own understanding. Proverbs 3:5 (ESV)

10 If you falter in a time of trouble, how small is your strength! Proverbs 24:10 (NIV)

Both the King of Syria and Elisha's servant were bogged down by what they saw in the natural, the things they believed were their only realities. Unlike Elisha, they could not see the manifestation of God's power in the spiritual realm, which was much stronger and more powerful than anything an earthly king could bring against him.

1 The Lord reigns, He is clothed with majesty; The Lord has clothed and girded Himself with strength; Indeed, the world is firmly established, it will not be moved. Psalm 93:1 (NASB)

37 For with God nothing shall be impossible. Luke 1:37 (KJV)

27 For the Lord of hosts has planned, and who can frustrate it? And as for His stretched-out hand, who can turn it back? Isaiah 14:27 (NASB)

In the natural, Elisha and his servant were surrounded by the forces of an angry king, with no hope of escape. The reality, however, was far different. In the same way, when we are confronted with difficult situations in our lives, no matter how hopelessly outmatched we appear to be in the natural, God's power in the spiritual realm is as strong on our behalf as it was on Elisha's.

God's armies and His hand of power did not stop moving some time in the Old Testament. Each of His promises is as potent for us today as it was for the prophet and his servant. What we must do is to pray for eyes to see the truth, that the presence of God encamped around our lives is stronger than any enemy we face. As Elijah said, I say to you today, *Fear not: for they that be with us are more than they that be with them.*

31 What, then, shall we say in response to these things? If God is for us, who can be against us? Romans 8:31 (NIV)

No matter what situation you face. No matter what challenge is around the next bend of your life. No matter how hopeless your job situation, doctor's report or family issues may appear, what you see in the natural is nothing compared to what God is willing to unleash on your behalf in the supernatural.

14 The Lord will fight for you, and you have only to be silent.
Exodus 14:14 (ESV)

Conflict, trouble, and adversity will reveal your sight plan. They expose your strengths as well as your weaknesses in relation your faith and reliance upon God. The crucible of testing reveals where your gaze is truly pointed.

The question is, what do you see today? Are your eyes so fixed on what you think you see in the natural realm that you're consumed with fear and doubt? Or, like Elisha, are you looking through eyes of faith at God's power in the spiritual realm of your life? May we all seek the Lord until our natural gaze is fully saturated with awareness of His supernatural power.

Questions for Contemplation

1. Think of an Elisha in your life, someone who always seems to see things differently from others. How does their perspective affect their behavior?

_____

_____

_____

_____

2. Why do you think most people, even Christians, have trouble seeing beyond the natural?

_____

_____

_____

_____

3. What is one area of your life that looks bleak by human standards?

_____

_____

_____

4. How would your perspective change if you saw God's army literally stationed around you, your home, or whatever area of difficulty you're thinking about?

_____

_____

_____

_____

5. The truth is, God's protection is no less real and available in your situation than it was in Elisha's. Write a prayer asking God to open your eyes, the way He opened the eyes of Elisha's servant, to see that His miraculous power is already encamped around you and your situation today.

_____

_____

_____

_____

Chapter 7

The Seventh Turn: Choosing Faith

Everyone walking the Christian walk does not have the same ability to see through spiritual eyes of faith. In the natural, some have no need of glasses to improve their ability to see; they have perfect vision. However, many do need the help of glasses or contacts to improve vision. In the same way, for some Christians, seeing through eyes of faith comes more easily than for others. By God's grace, however, every Christian has the potential for 20/20 faith-vision. In this chapter, we'll explore how to go from faithless to faith-filled living.

First of all, there's the "O Ye of Little Faith" sight plan. Then there's the "O Ye of Great Faith" sight plan. Whichever one you adhere to will dictate how you deal with the storms of life.

The "O Ye of Little Faith" plan is the one that says, as long as we are sailing along in calm waters, with no friction, no battle or struggles, just keeping it simple, all is well. You know, the times of no trouble, no issues or conflicts with people. These are the no hurt, pain or sickness folks, those who run from confrontations and the alignment processes that are needful and necessary for growth and development.

During seasons of serious turbulence, when things go wrong, they shout out, "It's the devil," or they play the blame game of, "It's always someone else's fault that I am going through what I am going through." Without faith, they are unable to see that many difficulties are blessings in disguise, spiritual tools of realignment.

These people are known for throwing in the towel, quitters they are. They bail out, walk out and fall out when the strong winds of storms and raging waters of life come. Anything that challenges the plan and mission of their family, ministry or business exposes their lack of trust and faith in God. They seek out worldly solutions and live in compromise. They attempt to fill spiritual voids with carnal substances, which leaves them empty and frustrated.

> *26 And he saith unto them, Why are ye fearful, O ye of little faith? Then he arose, and rebuked the winds and the sea; and there was a great calm.* Matthew 8:26 (KJV)

> *30 Wherefore, if God so clothe the grass of the field, which today is, and tomorrow is cast into the oven, shall he not much more clothe you, O ye of little faith?* Matthew 6:30 (KJV)

Then there's the "O Ye of Great Faith" sight plan. When life experiences, at times, do not look like what God has spoken, those with this plan choose to hold on to the Word of God and press their way into victory. They refuse to lie down without fighting the good fight of faith. Their song and motto is "I am trusting God no matter what!"

> *17 So then faith cometh by hearing, and hearing by the word of God.* Romans 10:17 (KJV)

> *God is not man, that he should lie, or a son of man, that he should change his mind. Has he said, and will he not do it? Or has he spoken, and will he not fulfill it?* Numbers 23:19 (ESV)

Achieving this faith-filled outlook comes when a person truly realizes that they are not in the fight of life by themselves and that somehow, some way the Lord is going to see them through. It's not dependent on outward circumstances; it comes from the inward assurance that God is in control.

Keen faith-vision is acquired by much study and meditation on the Word of God. Allowing the Word to become who you are and what you do is vital as you journey along in life. Satan is coming, but you must stand your ground and have faith in God's Word and divine ability to carry you through whatever comes your way.

> *8 Study this Book of Instruction continually. Meditate on it day and night so you will be sure to obey everything written in it. Only then will you prosper and succeed in all you do.* Joshua 1:8 (NLT)

> *24 Everyone then who hears these words of mine and does them will be like a wise man who built his house on the rock. 25 And the rain fell, and the floods came, and the winds blew and beat on that house, but it did not fall, because it had been founded on the rock. 26 And everyone who hears these words of mine and does not do them will be like a foolish man who built his house on the sand. 27 And the rain fell, and the floods came, and the winds blew and beat against that house, and it fell, and great was the fall of it.* Matthew 7:24-27 (ESV)

Recall the story of Elisha and his servant from the previous chapter. Think about yourself. What do you see when you encounter trouble and experience the unexpected? Like the servant, do you lose hope? Do you retreat and run to the mountains for cover or to the cave and live in fear and failure?

In contrast, are you like Elisha? Do you stand on what you believe, come hell or high water, and proclaim that God is more than able to save, heal and deliver? Remember, even though the servant was "seeing perfectly" from a natural standpoint, his vision was flawed; he needed the additional component of faith to be able to see what was really going on in the spiritual realm.

The most important question is: Has God changed His mind about what he has promised to do in your life because of what you're going through? And the answer is: God changes not!

> *6 I am the Lord, and I do not change. That is why you descendants of Jacob are not already destroyed.* Malachi 3:6 (NLT)

> *8 Jesus Christ is the same yesterday, today, and forever.* Hebrews 13:8 (NLT)

Seasons change and people change, but God does not. With that said, no one is exempt from going through or having to deal with life issues. Life issues hit every house, no matter what title or office you hold. You may be a bishop, movie star, CEO, janitor or worker at McDonalds, but regardless, you will have to deal with the issues of life. If you are married, single, have children or not, live in a mansion or a hut, you will have issues to deal with. Nobody gets a free ride.

> *1 Man that is born of a woman is of few days and full of trouble.* Job 14:1 (KJV)

If your so-called "faith" is only intact when things are going well, it's fair-weather faith, and that isn't faith at all. Real faith perseveres through trouble, seeing beyond what is visible in the natural realm to apprehend the spiritual truth that God is present and active in every situation.

> *1 Now faith is confidence in what we hope for and assurance about what we do not see.* Hebrews 11:1 (NIV)

24 Anyone who listens to my teaching and follows it is wise, like a person who builds a house on solid rock. 25 Though the rain comes in torrents and the floodwaters rise and the winds beat against that house, it won't collapse because it is built on bedrock. 26 But anyone who hears my teaching and doesn't obey it is foolish, like a person who builds a house on sand. 27 When the rains and floods come and the winds beat against that house, it will collapse with a mighty crash. Matthew 7:24-27 (NLT)

Because of our relationship with Christ, we have the power and the divine support to withstand the storms of life and the battles that come. We must believe, as the Scripture says:

13 For I can do everything through Christ, who gives me strength. Philippians 4:13 (NLT)

13 Wherefore take unto you the whole armour of God, that ye may be able to withstand in the evil day, and having done all, to stand. Ephesian 6:13 (KJV)

Questions for Contemplation

1. Do you wear glasses or contacts? What would happen if you decided to stop wearing them? How would your life be affected? If not, think about someone you know who uses vision correction. What happens when they take off their lenses?

_____

_____

_____

2. What about your faith-lenses? Are you seeing clearly, or is your life distorted by a lack of spiritual vision?

_____

_____

_____

_____

3. Recall a specific time when you had the "O Ye of Little Faith" sight plan. What happened?

_____

_____

_____

_____

4. Now, recall a specific time when you had the "O Ye of Great Faith" sight plan. How was that time different?

_____

_____

_____

_____

5. Take a moment to evaluate. No Christian has a perfect sight plan 100% of the time, but is the majority of your life lived with clear, faith-filled spiritual vision, or do you struggle to maintain your faith when things get tough? Write out a short prayer asking God to increase your faith.

_____

_____

_____

_____

Chapter 8

The Eighth Turn: Overcoming Obstacles
on the Path

There was a season in my life when the things that were visible in the natural were not all that there was to behold. I found an obstacle in front of me on my path, and I had the choice to trust God to help me through or to become discouraged and stop in the middle of the road.

> *Therefore, put on every piece of God's armor so you will be able to resist the enemy in the time of evil. Then after the battle you will still be standing firm.* Ephesians 6:13 (NLT)

Some years ago, when I was traveling and doing the work of ministry, my wife and I visited a friend's church in Ft. Lauderdale. He had booked a well-known evangelist to preach. The service was powerful, and God moved mightily. We decided to drive the two hours back home across Alligator Alley. We talked and laughed through the trip, but arrived home very late, at nearly 3:00 a.m.

Upon our arrival, I suddenly began to feel strangely ill. I began to feel very cold, not just a little cold, but I felt like I was on the Polar Express. I asked my wife to bring me a pair of socks. A short while after putting on the socks, I was still cold. I asked her to bring me some sweatpants, and she did. I put on the pants, but I continued to

73

shake and shiver. My teeth were chattering, and my body shook with violent chills. After I had asked for not one, but two, blankets, my wife became concerned and called the hospital. She spoke quickly to the nurse on the other end, and her answers brought about enough concern that the nurse finally said, "Bring him into the ER."

My wife drove me to the hospital, and after a few moments in triage, I was found to have a temperature of 105 degrees. The doctors came in and began asking more serious questions. I answered everything, but their concern increased, and they sent me through a battery of tests.

I sat quietly in a bed as they were waiting for the results of the first round of tests. While I sat, my wife noticed that I began to slump on the left side. As we talked, she tried to adjust me in the bed to sit up straight, but I could not maintain my own balance. Alarmed, she called for the nurse, who rushed in and said, "He is having a stroke."

My wife and the medical professionals began to talk to me and ask me questions. I couldn't remember the simplest things. There was no organization in my brain, but there was plenty of organization in my spirit. I told my wife, "We are going to do this." My spirit saw through eyes of faith, even as my mind was impaired.

> *1 Now faith is confidence in what we hope for and assurance about what we do not see. 2 This is what the ancients were commended for. 3 By faith we understand that the universe was formed at God's command, so that what is seen was not made out of what was visible.* Hebrews 11:1-3 (NIV)

Many people, at a juncture like this, freak out, pass out and even walk out, but I was not afraid. It's all about what you see and what you know. The surgery my illness required was successful, and I was placed in rehab. The doctors said recovery would be prolonged, but I was released from the hospital in record time.

A couple of weeks after the surgery, I noticed swelling in my incision area. I went to the doctor to have the surgical site checked out, and as he touched the area, it burst open like something in a zombie movie. I was facing a setback in my healing process. Even after the miracles God had performed in preserving my life and helping me through surgery, I still had to stand firm against the obstacle in my way.

I was frustrated as I learned that I would have to go to the hospital daily for six weeks to kill the staph infection in my incision, but I learned that I wasn't in this fight by myself. I had to believe that somehow, some way, God would bring me through, even when my way seemed blocked. I had to trust what my spiritual eyes saw, not my physical eyes, clinging to the promises found in God's Word. I slowly recovered and was eventually able to make a full turnaround.

This was a turning point for me. When you have to walk through the arena of contrary situations, opposition, conflict and a season of setbacks, you must maintain divine perception. Natural, human perception sees what the enemy is doing; divine perception sees that God is in control.

Matthew 6:25-34 (ESV)

25 Therefore I tell you, do not be anxious about your life, what you will eat or what you will drink, nor about your body, what you will put on. Is not life more than food, and the body more than clothing?

26 Look at the birds of the air: they neither sow nor reap nor gather into barns, and yet your heavenly Father feeds them. Are you not of more value than they?

27 And which of you by being anxious can add a single hour to his span of life?

28 And why are you anxious about clothing? Consider the lilies of the field, how they grow: they neither toil nor spin,

29 yet I tell you, even Solomon in all his glory was not arrayed like one of these.

30 But if God so clothes the grass of the field, which today is alive and tomorrow is thrown into the oven, will he not much more clothe you, O you of little faith?

31 Therefore do not be anxious, saying, 'What shall we eat?' or 'What shall we drink?' or 'What shall we wear?'

32 For the Gentiles seek after all these things, and your heavenly Father knows that you need them all.

33 But seek first the kingdom of God and his righteousness, and all these things will be added to you.

34 Therefore do not be anxious about tomorrow, for tomorrow will be anxious for itself. Sufficient for the day is its own trouble.

At times, we will all find ourselves surrounded by enemy forces that take on the appearance of major conflicts and adversity that is tougher than ever before. There will be times when those around you will not envision what you see or believe what you believe. Pray for those who walk with you along this journey, that their eyes will be open to see the presence of God in every situation.

As we read in a previous chapter, Elisha stood in the place of confidence and assurance that whatever situation arose, he would never be in the battle by himself. He refused to allow his condition or situation to change his consciousness of his position in God. Another biblical character, Paul, was also perpetually aware of a holy presence with him as he would go forth doing that which pleased God. As the Lord was with him, He is with us.

I am reminded of the profound words of the Apostle Paul as he walked out his journey in fulfilling the will of God. The book of Acts states this most defining moment of a man who has, in many ways, inspired me to become the servant that I am. Paul expressed a powerful declaration:

> *22 And now, behold, I go bound in the spirit unto Jerusalem, not knowing the things that shall befall me there: 23 Save that the Holy Ghost witnesseth in every city, saying that bonds and afflictions abide me. 24 But none of these things move me, neither count I my life dear unto myself, so that I might finish my course with joy, and the ministry, which I have received of the Lord Jesus, to testify the gospel of the grace of God.* Acts 20:22-24 (KJV)

I am astounded by this man's ability to remain focused, even while knowing that conflict and suffering awaited him at his next destination. More than anything else, he realized that he was going "bound in the spirit" to Jerusalem. He was spiritually empowered and spiritually driven.

Paul was completely sold out, and he knew that there would be difficulties and challenges. He was willing to go on, knowing that he was not in this fight by himself. He would never face any obstacle or adversity in his own strength or be forced to rely on his own abilities to save him. When we grasp the attitude that Paul had, seeing and knowing that we are never alone, we can conquer every obstacle, and we will succeed on the journey of faith.

> *13 No, dear brothers and sisters, I have not achieved it, but I focus on this one thing: Forgetting the past and looking forward to what lies ahead, 14 I press on to reach the end of the race and receive the heavenly prize for which God, through Christ Jesus, is calling us.* Philippians 3:13-14 (NLT)

Questions for Contemplation

1. Think of a time in your own life when you were confronted with an unexpected obstacle in your path. What were your first thoughts?

_____

_____

_____

_____

2. Once you had time to process the situation, how did you react?

_____

_____

_____

_____

3. How did your faith (or lack of faith) affect your situation?

_____

_____

_____

_____

4. Life on earth is never without challenges. What obstacle(s) is in your path right now?

_____

_____

_____

_____

5. God is much less interested in good circumstances than He is in good responses. Are you looking at your current situation with trust in God's faithfulness, or has your faith faltered? Today can be the first day of your new outlook. Write out a statement of commitment to trust God for your situation from this day forward.

_____

_____

_____

_____

Chapter 9

The Ninth Turn: Overcoming the Cycle

Seasons are an inescapable part of life, whether we're talking about the weather or about the personal ups and downs that fill our days from birth to death. Everyone experiences personal seasons of joy, loss, and everything in between. If we're open to God's leading, the cycles and seasons of our lives become times of growth that propel us to greater heights of faith and accomplishment.

1 There is a time for everything,

and a season for every activity under the heavens:

2 a time to be born and a time to die,

a time to plant and a time to uproot,

3 a time to kill and a time to heal,

a time to tear down and a time to build,

4 a time to weep and a time to laugh,

a time to mourn and a time to dance,

5 a time to scatter stones and a time to gather them,

a time to embrace and a time to refrain from embracing,

6 a time to search and a time to give up,

a time to keep and a time to throw away,

7 a time to tear and a time to mend,

a time to be silent and a time to speak,

8 a time to love and a time to hate,

a time for war and a time for peace.

Ecclesiastes 3:1-8 (NIV)

The problem is, many people fail to let their life's cycles teach them anything. They doom themselves to repeat the same lessons over and over because they settle for what is comfortable and familiar instead of reaching for what is eternal and transcendent.

Remember the Children of Israel, God's chosen people? For forty years, they wandered in the desert, covering and re-covering the same ground because of their failure to have faith in God's promises. God's desire was to take them into the Promised Land, but instead they repeated the same cycle over and over, turning to false gods and discouragement because they chose to sink into their fear of the enemies in front of them.

2 All the Israelites grumbled against Moses and Aaron, and the whole assembly said to them, If only we had died in Egypt! Or in this wilderness! 3 Why is the Lord bringing us to this land only to let us fall by the sword? Our wives and children will be taken as plunder. Wouldn't it be better for us to go back to Egypt? 4 And they said to each other, 'We should choose a leader and go back to Egypt.' Numbers 14:2-4 (NIV)

The Israelites didn't have the power to control all of their circumstances or to keep trials from happening to them, but they did have the choice to either settle into what they perceived in the natural realm or to choose to put their faith in the God they could not see. Unfortunately, they made the wrong choice, and it had dire consequences for the whole nation.

Numbers 14:21-31 (NIV)

21 Nevertheless, as surely as I live and as surely as the glory of the Lord fills the whole earth,

22 not one of those who saw my glory and the signs I performed in Egypt and in the wilderness but who disobeyed me and tested me ten times—

23 not one of them will ever see the land I promised on oath to their ancestors. No one who has treated me with contempt will ever see it.

24 But because my servant Caleb has a different spirit and follows me wholeheartedly, I will bring him into the land he went to, and his descendants will inherit it.

25 Since the Amalekites and the Canaanites are living in the valleys, turn back tomorrow and set out toward the desert along the route to the Red Sea.

26 The Lord said to Moses and Aaron:

27 'How long will this wicked community grumble against me? I have heard the complaints of these grumbling Israelites.'

28 So tell them, 'As surely as I live, declares the Lord, I will do to you the very thing I heard you say:

29 In this wilderness your bodies will fall—every one of you twenty years old or more who was counted in the census and who has grumbled against me.

30 Not one of you will enter the land I swore with uplifted hand to make your home, except Caleb son of Jephunneh and Joshua son of Nun.

31 As for your children that you said would be taken as plunder, I will bring them in to enjoy the land you have rejected.

As you can see in the above passage, Caleb and Joshua were spared from God's judgment, because they chose to put faith in God's promises to help His people take possession of the Promised Land. The rest of the Israelites sank into the cycle; Joshua and Caleb transcended it through their faith in God. All of the Israelites went through the experience; only two made the right choice about how to respond to it.

Today, we have the same choice. We all endure seasons and cycles, but some people get stuck, and others transcend. Why is this? Everyone has challenges in life, related to upbringing, culture, toxic relationships, or a host of other things, many of which are handed to us in childhood, before we're even old enough to know what's going on.

Some people become chronic settlers: They settle for the first offer, the codependent relationship, the routine they know is flawed but familiar. They follow the same unhealthy patterns of behavior over and over because they've settled for what is, instead of choosing to believe for what could be. Their eyes are fixed on their limitations and on the comfort zone of familiarity, even when that familiarity is twisted and negative.

Settlers look at new opportunities and say, "That's not for me." They abort the mission of their lives, not by doing anything big and dramatic, but instead by sitting where they are, going through the motions of the cycle, and never using what they go through to change and grow. Growth is challenging, and change can be difficult, but the alternative of sitting and settling while life passes us by is unacceptable. It's a slow, lazy process that atrophies our spiritual muscles and holds us back from experiencing the abundant adventure God has in store for each one of us.

Those who refuse to settle are people who lock in, go to prayer, and seek the Word of God for answers to their situation, no matter what season or cycle they find themselves experiencing. They see trials as opportunities for growth and their flaws as places of potential, where God's power can take human weakness and transform it into heavenly strength. Where the world sees foolishness, they see the wisdom of God, and through it their perspective is transformed.

At one point in time, our church, First Assembly Cornerstone, was faced with a season of serious financial challenge. With an unemployment rate of over thirty percent, our community did not seem like a place with the resources to meet the challenges we faced. In the natural, we were up against insurmountable odds.

However, we chose to look at our season through eyes of faith instead of getting bogged down in the human complications surrounding us. We refused to get comfortable with failure. Instead, we believed God for the divine provision He had promised in His Word.

In the middle of our community, with all the challenges our members and adherents face, we were able to turn our situation around by careful stewardship of God's miraculous provision. Within a few years, our season of challenge had turned into a season of overcoming. What seemed impossible in the natural was made possible by God's supernatural power, but we would never have experienced this miracle if we had chosen to accept the first report and settled for the human interpretation of our challenges.

As Christians, we are called to be cross-bearers, people who daily take up the glorious calling of looking beyond where we are now toward where God wants to take us. When the world says to settle for the darkness of our issues and our circumstances, we are called to be the light.

1 Corinthians 1:18-25 (NIV)

18 For the message of the cross is foolishness to those who are perishing, but to us who are being saved it is the power of God.

19 For it is written: 'I will destroy the wisdom of the wise; the intelligence of the intelligent I will frustrate.'

20 Where is the wise person? Where is the teacher of the law? Where is the philosopher of this age? Has not God made foolish the wisdom of the world?

21 For since in the wisdom of God the world through its wisdom did not know him, God was pleased through the foolishness of what was preached to save those who believe.

22 Jews demand signs and Greeks look for wisdom,

23 but we preach Christ crucified: a stumbling block to Jews and foolishness to Gentiles,

24 but to those whom God has called, both Jews and Greeks, Christ the power of God and the wisdom of God.

25 For the foolishness of God is wiser than human wisdom, and the weakness of God is stronger than human strength.

"Good enough" is not good enough, and "just because I've always done it this way" is no answer to the challenges of life. We must be people of faith, who choose to learn through the seasons of our lives, rather than mindlessly being controlled by our habits and hangups. God's plan for each of us is far greater than anywhere we've been so far.

Questions for Contemplation

1. How would you describe the current season of your life?

_____

_____

_____

_____

2. Imagine being an Israelite. How do you think you would have responded to the dangerous circumstances in the Promised Land? Would you have held onto God's promises like Joshua and Caleb did, or would you have lost faith like most of the Israelites did?

_____

_____

_____

_____

3. List an area (or areas) of your life in which you seem to repeat the same cycle of problems or mistakes over and over.

_____

_____

_____

_____

4. Are you ready to take the faith steps necessary to let God move you past your familiar patterns? (Be honest)

_____

_____

_____

_____

5. Write out a prayer of faith asking God to help you learn the lesson and move through whatever season you're experiencing. Or, if you answered "no" to the question above, write a prayer asking God to help you reach a place of readiness to step out of your comfort zone.

_____

_____

_____

_____

Chapter 10

The Tenth Turn:
It Doesn't Have to End This Way

No matter where you find yourself today, your journey doesn't have to end here. Nowhere is too far, too difficult, or too insurmountable for God to reach you, and His plan can turn every mistake and misfortune into a blessing in your life. ***Giving up is not an option, and victory is ahead, no matter where you are right now.***

Maybe you're just beginning this journey, a newcomer to faith. No pursuit in life will ever be as rewarding as this one. Commitment to Christ is the key to unlocking your full potential and setting you on the course for absolute victory. Regardless of where you come from or what you've been through, in God, you are a new creation, and your success is assured.

17 Therefore, if anyone is in Christ, he is a new creation. The old has passed away; behold, the new has come. 18 All this is from God, who through Christ reconciled us to himself and gave us the ministry of reconciliation; 19 that is, in Christ God was reconciling the world to himself, not counting their trespasses against them, and entrusting to us the message of reconciliation. 20 Therefore, we are ambassadors for Christ, God making his appeal through us. We implore you on behalf

*of Christ, be reconciled to God. 21 For our sake he made him
to be sin who knew no sin, so that in him we might become
the righteousness of God.* 2 Corinthians 5:17-21 (ESV)

Maybe you took a bad turn a while ago. Maybe it's been a long time since you were on the right path, heading toward the finish line. If you're in a negative place in life, at a point that isn't God-honoring, take heart: God is the God of the turnaround. He delights in lovingly forgiving us and bringing us home to His heart. If you trust Him, He will lead you back to a place of security in His will.

> *1 I waited patiently for the Lord;*
> *he inclined to me and heard my cry.*
> *2 He drew me up from the pit of destruction,*
> *out of the miry bog,*
> *and set my feet upon a rock,*
> *making my steps secure.*
> *3 He put a new song in my mouth,*
> *a song of praise to our God.*
> *Many will see and fear,*
> *and put their trust in the Lord.*
>
> *Psalm 40:1-3 (ESV)*

Maybe you're discouraged and weary in well-doing. Don't despair. **You can do this!** No matter how much it costs, no matter how big it is, no matter what it takes. God will see you through to the finish line if you're committed to going the distance. Even Jesus had times of weariness, but instead of giving up, He pressed into His Father's strength. If you follow His example, praying and studying the Word, you will find reserves of strength that you never could have imagined.

*9 And let us not be weary in well doing: for in due season we
shall reap, if we faint not.* Galatians 6:9 (KJV)

15 But the news about Him was spreading farther, and large crowds kept gathering to hear Him and to be healed of their illnesses. 16 But Jesus Himself would often slip away to the wilderness and pray [in seclusion]. Luke 5:15-16 (AMP)

13 I can do all things [which He has called me to do] through Him who strengthens and empowers me [to fulfill His purpose—I am self-sufficient in Christ's sufficiency; I am ready for anything and equal to anything through Him who infuses me with inner strength and confident peace.] Philippians 4:13 (AMP)

Maybe you're on the cusp of growth, trying to be patient while God's plan is brought to fruition in your life. Just keep saying it until you see it. Keep preparing with faith. Put your business, family, ministry, and health into the hands of God. If you try to take control and force things to happen before God's perfect timing, you will reap frustration. Only He knows the exact right moment to release you into new opportunities. Remember, we may not be where we're going, but we're not where we were.

14 Wait on the Lord: be of good courage, and he shall strengthen thine heart: wait, I say, on the Lord. Psalm 27:14 (KJV)

34 Wait for the Lord and keep his way, and he will exalt you to inherit the land; you will look on when the wicked are cut off. Psalm 37:34 (ESV)

31 But they that wait upon the Lord shall renew their strength; they shall mount up with wings as eagles; they shall run, and not be weary; and they shall walk, and not faint. Isaiah 40:31 (KJV)

Maybe you're in a good place. Perhaps you're tempted to settle where you are because you like the view. Rest is a good thing, but stopping and settling for the status quo is deadly. There's no stasis in a life with God: We either move forward by faith, or we will slide backward. Be encouraged; God is not finished with you. He has more turns, seasons, and dreams up ahead for your life. Let him take you further, leading you ever onward in Him.

"Live your dreams" can be a cliched phrase, used without much real meaning or real significance. Those of us on the path of life with Christ, however, know that it's a deep concept, and it's not easy. Dreams that God plants in us are more than ideas in our minds. They are tangible, vital goals that He has created us to reach.

> *35 So do not throw away your confidence; it will be richly rewarded. 36 You need to persevere so that when you have done the will of God, you will receive what he has promised.*
> Hebrews 10:35-36 (NIV)

The world's idea of dreams is a prideful and self-centered one, based in ideals of achievement for personal gain and grasping as much as possible. Often, it's about advancing at the expense of others, in our own strength and in our own time.

> *21 Many are the plans in a person's heart, but it is the Lord's purpose that prevails.* Proverbs 19:21 (NIV)

God-given dreams are quite different. They're things we could never do on our own, that we must depend on Him to achieve through us, with our effort and cooperation. Like children first learning to form letters, we need God's hands around ours, guiding each mark we make. These divine goals are not only for our benefit, but they also have the potential to touch the world. Dreams give us hope to keep going, to leave our issues behind, and to embrace God's purposes in our lives.

If people can't see what God is doing,
they stumble all over themselves;
But when they attend to what he reveals,
they are most blessed. Proverbs 29:18 (MSG)

Of course, the Christian life is not a solitary one. God blesses our journey so that we, in turn, can bless others with what we've learned. As you grow with God, look out for brothers and sisters next to you on the path. It may be that God will lead you to becomes a mentor for someone else.

11 Follow my example, as I follow the example of Christ.
1 Corinthians 11:1 (NIV)

Today is the day to begin again, to entrust your life fully into God's hands and watch to see the miracles He will do through every turn along the path. Don't hesitate. Your journey has only just begun.

20 He said to them, 'Because of your little faith. For truly, I say to you, if you have faith like a grain of mustard seed, you will say to this mountain, 'Move from here to there,' and it will move, and nothing will be impossible for you.' Matthew 17:20 (ESV)

33 But first and most importantly seek (aim at, strive after) His kingdom and His righteousness [His way of doing and being right—the attitude and character of God], and all these things will be given to you also. Matthew 6:33 (AMP)

Questions for Contemplation

1. This chapter talks about several different places on the path of life. Which one is closest to where you find yourself?

_____

_____

_____

2. Do you really believe God wants to lead you to a new place in Him? Why or why not?

_____

_____

_____

_____

3. Describe one dream in your heart that you believe is from God.

_____

_____

_____

_____

4. How would your life change if you truly believed that nothing in your life is impossible with God? Write out Philippians 4:13 in the translation of your choice, and if you have not committed it to memory, memorize it this week.

_____

_____

_____

_____

5. When you're ready, write a final prayer committing your journey to God from this day forward.

_____

_____

_____

_____

Afterword: Joseph's Story

God's divine transportation is God getting us from one place to another place that's really the expected end that He originally intended. it's moving from the place of seeing the dream or vision of your life to getting to the place of fulfillment and manifestation. Throughout this book, we've looked at many turning points and choices along the way. Now let's look at the hand of God moving supernaturally through the life of one of His servants.

The story of Joseph is the perfect biblical example of God's divine transportation. When people look at the Joseph story, many see the relationship of a father and his favorite son through the coat of many colors. Some focus on the sibling rivalry between the baby boy and his older brothers. Others focus only on the family's dysfunctional realities, the same types that exist in many families within our communities and nation. Some see the seed of the promise looking not so promising; however, like many of us, the characters in this story are works in progress, not yet at their final destination even though they were anointed and appointed.

Through the progression of Joseph's life and journey, we see the aggressive development of the seeds of anger and jealousy. These seeds can drive the ones who should be loving you to actually abuse you and even attempt to destroy you. However, when the sovereign will of God is revealed, His purposes and promises are fulfilled, no matter the mistakes and wrongs people have committed.

God's divine transportation took the deep frustrations and hidden agendas of Joseph's brothers and used them to place him in his prophetic destiny. We must take a moment to reflect on the dream that Joseph shared with his brothers, the dream that one day, the sun and the moon and the eleven stars would bow down to him and give homage to him. His brothers could not image such a thing ever happening, and they became offended and insulted due to his dream.

> *5 Now Joseph had a dream, and when he told it to his brothers they hated him even more. 6 He said to them, 'Hear this dream that I have dreamed: 7 Behold, we were binding sheaves in the field, and behold, my sheaf arose and stood upright. And behold, your sheaves gathered around it and bowed down to my sheaf.' 8 His brothers said to him, 'Are you indeed to reign over us? Or are you indeed to rule over us?' So they hated him even more for his dreams and for his words.*
> Genesis 37:5-8 (ESV)

Now, after some time had passed, the father sent Joseph on assignment to check on the status of his brothers who were supposed to be in one place working, but were actually in another place playing around. Then, after they realized that Joseph knew of their doings and whereabouts, they decided to get rid of the talebearer. They seized their brother and put him in a pit to eventually die, but later regretted the decision and went to retrieve Joseph; however, Joseph was not there. He had been taken by the traveling merchants during the night and was en route, through God's divine transportation, into Egypt. Remember, divine transportation is God getting us from one place to another, to the expected end and prophetic destiny.

Joseph was transported to Egypt under the cover name of slave. It would seem as though he was in enemy hands and in the land of the enemy, but he was really in the vehicle of God's divine transportation. I must add that while under the cover of a slave, the favor of God was still on his life. From an outside perspective, it looks as though this story is about a young man's life that has gone bust and is now headed down the pathway of a disastrous conclusion. Nevertheless, there are times when God allows some things to go wrong in order that His predestined will prevails. Joseph was traveling in the vehicle, not of his own will, but of the will of God.

Once he reached Egypt, things were not getting any better for Joseph, but worse. One day, he has the favor of his master Potiphar, and the next day, he's falsely accused of sexual assault by his master's wife. One day, he's a slave in his master's house, in charge of its operations, and another day he's in prison serving a sentence for a crime he didn't commit. Even when things go from bad to worse, God is not going to allow your purpose to be ambushed and destroyed, because He is yet working things out for your good. The enemy has plots, but God has a plan. What the enemy threw at you as a stone of hindrance, God will use to get you to the next phase of your prophetic destiny, just as He did with Joseph.

> *20 And Joseph's master took him and put him into the prison, the place where the king's prisoners were confined, and he was there in prison. 21 But the Lord was with Joseph and showed him steadfast love and gave him favor in the sight of the keeper of the prison. 22 And the keeper of the prison put Joseph in charge of all the prisoners who were in the prison. Whatever was done there, he was the one who did it. 23 The keeper of the prison paid no attention to anything that was in Joseph's charge, because the Lord was with him. And whatever he did, the Lord made it succeed.* Genesis 39:20-23 (ESV)

While Joseph was in prison, God created a situation that exposed a gift within him and would eventually make room for him to stand before royalty. The chief baker and chief wine steward. who served the Pharaoh, had somehow, because of misconduct, angered the Pharaoh and were thrown into the jail where the prisoners were being held under the royal guard. One night, they both had dreams that deeply troubled them, for they were without interpretation of the matter. Joseph noticed their change of countenance and inquired of them, "Why are you looking so distressed?" They shared with Joseph about their troubled dreams.

Joseph interpreted their dreams as the Lord gave him the interpretation, and the interpretation revealed that one of them would live to return to the palace and serve the Pharaoh once again, while the other would be sentenced to die. There was one request asked of the one who would return to his previous assignment in the Pharaoh's palace, and that was to remember the kindness of Joseph.

Two years passed, and no word from the palace arrived, but in the fullness of time, the Pharaoh had a disturbing dream, and there was no one in his house—sorcerer, magician, or astrologer—who could discern or interpret his dream. Then the servant who had been in the prison with Joseph remembered the gift that had blessed him and the promise he had given Joseph to remember him. Now the time had come for Joseph to move through God's divine transportation into the palace.

Genesis 41:37-43 (ESV)

> *37 This proposal pleased Pharaoh and all his servants.*
>
> *38 And Pharaoh said to his servants, 'Can we find a man like this, in whom is the Spirit of God?'*
>
> *39 Then Pharaoh said to Joseph, 'Since God has shown you all this, there is none so discerning and wise as you are.*
>
> *40 You shall be over my house, and all my people shall order themselves as you command.[d] Only as regards the throne will I be greater than you.'*

41 And Pharaoh said to Joseph, 'See, I have set you over all the land of Egypt.' 42 Then Pharaoh took his signet ring from his hand and put it on Joseph's hand, and clothed him in garments of fine linen and put a gold chain about his neck.

43 And he made him ride in his second chariot. And they called out before him, 'Bow the knee!' Thus he set him over all the land of Egypt.

Through the years, I have heard messages from this text that spoke of one moving from the pit to the palace, from rags to riches. As I look into this story, I see God's divine transportation moving into the life of His servant to bring him into his expected end. I see all things working out for the good of them that love God, them who are called according to His purpose. I see God's divine transportation transporting His servant through purpose, process and promise.

If you are God's child, you are no less loved than Joseph, and God's plan for your life is equally certain. Despite the challenges Joseph faced, God's divine transportation was always at work in his life, bringing about God's perfect plan at the right time. Whether or not you can see it, God's divine transportation is also at work in your life, taking all of your twists and turns along the way and working them into His perfect plan.

11 'For I know the plans I have for you,' declares the LORD, 'plans to prosper you and not to harm you, plans to give you hope and a future.' Jeremiah 29:11 (NIV)

About the Author

Anointed, appointed, radical, yet mild tempered are some words to describe Pastor Gregory Ford, Man of Faith & Power who preaches the Word without fear or favoritism. Pastor Ford holds a Bachelor's Degree in Theology from Life Christian University and is currently pursuing his Master's Degree. He is an ordained minister of the Assemblies of God, as well as being a fifteen-year Affiliate Member of the Potter's House International Pastoral Alliance under Bishop T.D. Jakes. His published works include the books *The Journey from No Man to God's Man* and **Get to the Point.**

He is a Pastor with an Evangelist call upon his life but yet operates in the totality of the Five-fold ministry. Winning Souls and being used to transform the lives of God's people is his mandate; he has been called into the kingdom for such a time as this, to set the prisoners free from sinful bondage. Gregory Ford accepted Jesus Christ into his life at an early age. Like most young people, challenges did arise… BUT GOD!

The Effectual Fervent Prayers of his Mother did avail much. During his upbringing, many great mentors and apostolic leaders poured into the life of the man of God, releasing him into ministry as he operated around the Nation as an Evangelist declaring and preaching the unadulterated and uncompromising Word of God.

In 1992, Pastor Ford began his pastoral tenure as the Senior Pastor of True Hope Pentecostal Church, located in Immokalee, Florida. After years of faithfully laboring in True Hope's ministry as

Pastor and Evangelist, by the prompting of the Holy Spirit, he was directed to step out and walk the vision God had placed in his heart. In 1997, Pastor Ford, his family and a group of devoted Christians, formally proclaimed the Vision of Anointed Word Deliverance Center, which was also located in Immokalee Florida. Gregory Ford is More than a Man with a Microphone… He is a Man with a Mission of a Kingdom Mandate.

By Divine intervention… purpose met destiny, and on October 4, 2004 a new chapter in the ministry of Gregory Ford began as he became the lead campus pastor for First Assembly Cornerstone located in Fort Myers, FL. While under the Leadership of Pastor Ford, First Assembly Cornerstone has become a place of refuge and safety for many and has made a divine impact in the community and surrounding areas.

This is all for the Glory of God and the building of the Kingdom of God. Behind every Great Man there is an anointed Help-mate. Pastor Ford is married to Marjorie, who serves as his Co-Pastor of First Assembly Cornerstone. Pastor Ford is also the Father of Four Children, a Family Man indeed. God has Proven Himself Strong and Mighty in the lives of the Fords. Transitioning into Destiny was not without small and sometimes testing beginnings. For Gregory Ford, it has always been, "…all about the Kingdom, and doing those things that please God."

CPSIA information can be obtained
at www.ICGtesting.com
Printed in the USA
LVOW10*1143230517
534971LV00003BA/4/P